FINDING THE RIGHT WORDS

Offering Care and Comfort
When You Don't Know What to Say

Wilfred Bockelman

AUGSBURG ■ Minneapolis

FINDING THE RIGHT WORDS
Offering Care and Comfort When You Don't Know What to Say

Copyright © 1990 Augsburg Fortress. All rights reserved. Except for brief quotations in critical articles or reviews, no part of this book may be reproduced in any manner without prior written permission from the publisher. Write to: Permissions, Augsburg Fortress, 426 S. Fifth St., Box 1209, Minneapolis, MN 55440.

Scripture quotations unless otherwise noted are from the Holy Bible: New International Version. Copyright 1978 by the New York International Bible Society. Used by permission of Zondervan Bible Publishers.

Cover design: MacLean & Tuminelly

Library of Congress Cataloging-in-Publication Data
Bockelman, Wilfred.
    Finding the right words : offering care and comfort when you don't know what to say / Wilfred Bockelman.
      p.   cm.
    ISBN 0-8066-2444-2
    1. Consolation. 2. Caring. I. Title.
BV4905.2.B62   1990
248.8'6—dc20   89-14975
                                                 CIP

The paper used in this publication meets the minimum requirements of American National Standard for Information Sciences—Permanence of Paper for Printed Library Materials, ANSI Z329.48-1984. ∞™

Manufactured in the U.S.A.   AF 9-2444

99   98   97   96   95   7   8   9   10   11   12   13   14   15

Contents

Introduction

Three incidents prompted me to write this book.

The first of these incidents involved a friend whom I will call Jane and her friend Carol. For eight years Jane wanted to say something to Carol, but she couldn't find the right words.

Jane and Carol had been singing partners. Both were about the same age. Jane and her husband, Bill, had three boys. Carol completed college first and went on to earn a master's degree. That was a struggle, but now everything was upbeat for her. She and her husband had a beautiful marriage, and she was starting a career that she planned to continue after the baby she was carrying was a couple years old.

Then it happened: Carol was in an auto accident, and overnight she became a quadriplegic. She also lost the baby.

"I was absolutely devastated," Jane said, as she told the story eight years later. "I didn't go to see Carol in the hospital. I sent her cards, but I didn't go to see her, because *I didn't know what to say.*"

The second incident that gave rise to the decision to write this book concerned a young couple who had a

5

son who died in infancy from a rather bizarre accident. Recalling it a year later, the mother, who was my secretary at the time, said, "After it was all over, some of our best friends acted as though it just hadn't happened. It was not because they were insensitive, I'm sure. They probably thought that the whole thing was so painful to us that we didn't want to talk about it. They just didn't know what to say."

The third incident involved a friend who moved to another city. Whenever I made a business trip to that city, I would make it a point to spend an hour or so with him. During these conversations I would always ask about his wife, and he would ask about mine.

Then I stopped asking about his wife, for I had heard rumors that the two of them were not getting along too well and possibly even were divorced. *I didn't know what to say.*

After one of those visits I wrote to my friend about a business matter and added a personal paragraph:

I've got to say something, and you can decide if you want to respond or comment on it. I've been embarrassed about never asking how your wife is. I have heard you are divorced, but I'm not sure. I didn't know what to say. If you are divorced, that must have been painful, and I simply want to say that I care about you; and if there is anything you care to say, I'll be a willing listener.

My friend responded immediately:

Yes, my wife and I have been divorced. I know it's awkward to bring up the matter, for it's hard to know what to say. But sometimes saying, "I don't know what to say," is better than not saying anything at all. Why don't you write a book about not knowing what to say?

When we find ourselves in a situation similar to the one in which Jane unexpectedly found herself, we want to offer care and comfort, but we don't know what to say.

Being at a loss for words is not all bad. We need to remember that sometimes *we don't have to say anything*. The very fact that we are present in a time of crisis and thus showing our concern may be more meaningful than anything we say.

Asking "What do I say?" also provides an opportunity to be reminded that sometimes there is a much larger obligation than a one-time, quick verbal response. The situation may require a long-term relationship with a commitment to personal involvement.

Perhaps the best way to tell what this book is, is to say what it is not. The purpose of this book is not to make a professional counselor out of the reader. Although this book deals with such problems as death, terminal illness, and divorce, it is not intended to provide comprehensive answers for persons involved with these problems. Neither does it give simple answers with step-by-step instructions so that one can look up the topic he or she needs help with and find the precise words to say.

One problem in writing a book intended to be helpful to people is that people differ in very complex ways. For example, Americans in general seem to be practical people who don't want to be bothered with a lot of theory, who are uncomfortable with mystery. But, having said that, I quickly run into a lot of people who are the exact opposite of that stereotype. Increasingly America is becoming multicultural, and people from different cultural and ethnic backgrounds express themselves in a variety of ways when facing tragedy. People from certain religious backgrounds may have ways of responding to grief that are not readily understood or appreciated by others. Therefore, conclusions in this book, drawn mostly from my own experiences, will be helpful to some and not to others.

My hope, then, for this book is a very modest one: that it may be helpful to some—not that it will give all the answers, not even that it will be a study book. It would be a mistake either to try to give all the answers or to give no answers at all. I have chosen instead, on the basis of my own insights and the opinions of others who seem to be skilled at "finding the right words," to move the reader a little further along the way in finding words to say at critical moments.

We may never learn how to respond naturally. Perhaps we shouldn't. Perhaps the person who objected to this book being written was right: "It never *should* be easy for us to talk to someone who is going through tragedy," she said. "Why should we ever feel comfortable talking about death to a 35-year-old mother of four children who is terminally ill with cancer?"

Incidentally, the person who made that statement has subsequently died of cancer herself. And Jane, who finally did talk to Carol, found herself in a similar and equally tragic situation with another friend. "It doesn't get any easier," she said. "It is just as difficult the second time as the first."

Perhaps we are struggling over words. Maybe *easy* and *comfortable* are not the right words. But what we are talking about is developing a sensitive and caring attitude that prompts us to share ourselves with those who are living with various kinds of pain.

1

The Heart
of the Matter

This book could have begun with a theory and then gone on to the practical application of that theory. That is a typical and logical approach. Some would say that is the only way to begin, or at least the best way.

Many people like to get right to the heart of the matter: "Don't give me a lot of theory about why something should be done; just tell me how to do it. Help me learn what to say."

This chapter, then, will give a few suggestions to "get your feet wet" as you try to develop a greater skill in knowing what to say in awkward, embarrassing, or difficult situations. They are offered with the warning, however, that skill and sensitivity to know what to say do not come simply from memorizing answers to questions. Later chapters will deal with both questions and answers in greater depth.

Most tragedies come unannounced. The people who have them, like Carol, described in the introduction, who became a quadriplegic overnight, don't have time to prepare for them. Their friends, like Jane, are equally unprepared to respond and know what to say. Either they are on the scene and feel compelled, ready or not, to say something; or, like Jane, they find the whole experience so devastating that they keep silent for years, desperately wishing they knew what to say.

Deep down we know that genuine care-giving is more than just saying something, but we do look for words to say at the moment. Here, then, are some opening comments that can be made in specific situations:

■ When the 85-year-old father of a close friend has died: "It's hard, isn't it, even when we have known all along that this would happen. I remember so many happy times I had with your father."

■ When the elderly mother of a colleague has died. Your colleague is not even a close friend, and you didn't know her mother at all, but you are expected to call at the funeral home during visitation hours: "I never knew your mother, but I heard you talk about her once in a while at work. I remember from your comments that you had a close relationship. I'm sure you'll miss her."

■ When the spouse of an elderly person has died: "We have all been expecting this, but now that it's here, it's still hard. At least he [she] is at rest. How are *you* feeling?"

■ When a young or early-middle-aged parent leaves a spouse and children behind: "We'll never know why these things happen, will we? Just know that we have been thinking of you and praying for you. How are the children taking it? I know it is easy to say, 'If there is anything we can do, just let us know,' but I'll get back to you in a few days to see what I might do to be of help. Is there something special that I can do for you now, like doing some cleaning, cutting the grass, or anything like that?"

■ When a teenager has been killed in an accident: "Let me just hold you tight. Oh, how we loved him [her]! He [she] was such a fine young man [woman]. What a tragedy! God must be shedding tears, too."

■ When visiting a close friend already weak from terminal illness: "Joan, this is Vivian. Don't feel that you have to say anything. Just rest. I'd just like to be here with you for a while."

"Joyce, I remember you said once that you hoped you would live until spring so that you could hear the birds sing once more. Would you like me to open the window so that you can hear the birds sing?"

"Hello, Alice. I brought some flowers. They're from the women at the club. They've been asking about you. How are you doing?"

■ When you have just heard that a bright 14-year-old daughter of the family across the street from you has committed suicide: "I'm not here because I know what to say. I don't know what to say. I'm very, very sorry."

■ When a 34-year-old mother of two children has just been told that she has cancer and that it probably is terminal: "Jim has just told me what the doctor said. I can't possibly know how you feel except to know that it must be a terrible blow. If you want to talk about it, fine. But don't feel you have to. Just know that I care deeply about you."

■ When your closest friends, members of your bridge club, who you always thought had a good marriage, are getting a divorce: "I heard, and I'm sorry. I'm sure there must be pain. If it helps to talk about it, count me as a friend who is willing to listen and not pass judgment. If you don't want to talk about it, I'll respect that, too."

■ When your neighbor's unmarried teenage daughter is pregnant: "Mary, I heard about Jennifer. It must be difficult for all of you. You can count on our support. Is there any way at all that we can be of help?"

Obviously you should not go into a situation and repeat by rote the words that have just been suggested. There will be occasions when those words are not appropriate, but they at least are a jumping-off place from which further conversation can develop.

Situations vary, of course, and should be dealt with in different ways. You would say something different to a close friend who has just discovered that he or she has terminal illness than you would to an 86-year-old grandmother who really wants to die. You would say something different to parents who have just learned that their 13-year-old daughter has been killed in a motorcycle accident than you would to the surviving widow of a 70-year-old man whose death has been expected.

Nevertheless, there are some general principles that pertain to almost any situation. Here are four such guidelines:

1. *Even when you don't know what to say, go to the person who has had the tragedy.* Presence is important, but also be open to signals if the person wants to be alone. It is far better to say, "I don't know what to say," than not to go because you feel you won't know what to say. At times that may be the very best thing to say, because it shows that you share the deepest pain with them.

2. *Make it as easy as possible for the person to whom you are talking to say what he or she wants to say instead of doing all the talking yourself.* Be sure you have listened, not only with your ears, but with an awareness of and general sensitivity to the situation. Don't start by giving exhortations. Use leading questions to allow the person to whom you are speaking to give a clue as

to how much he or she wants to say. It is not always necessary to do a lot of talking. Just being present with a hug or a touch on the arm or a look into the other's eyes can be very strengthening.

A simple question such as "How did it happen?" or "Do you want to talk about it?" can give a clue as to whether the person is interested in talking at all or if a moment of silence is preferred.

3. *Don't promise anything you don't expect to fulfill.* Don't say, "If there is ever anything I can do, feel free to call on me," if you don't have any intention of doing anything if it would inconvenience you. Don't even say, "I'll pray for you," if in actuality you probably won't. When offering to do something, it is best to be specific. For instance, "I know you've got a lot of things to take care of. Would you like me to take your laundry home and do it for you?" Or "Why don't you just let me stay and help you do the dishes and vacuum the floor since a lot of people may be stopping in?" Or "Are there any errands I can run for you, like getting some groceries or taking the kids to their piano lessons?"

4. *Be prepared to follow through after the first shock of tragedy wears off.* The initial concern, of course, is to offer support for the immediate situation, but this is also a good time to make a commitment to be just as caring six weeks or six months or a year later, when the need may be just as great as now. In other words, a family that experiences the death of a husband and father will likely get ample attention at the time of the death and for a few weeks following. Now is the time to commit yourself not to forget the widow six months or a year from now or during special occasions or holidays when she will be especially lonely.

Some books list things one should *not* say at difficult times. Rather than being helpful, this "negative" advice makes the reader even more insecure in such situations. A grieving person knows that it is difficult for others to express themselves and usually is very understanding when someone is awkward in communicating his or her feelings. This is illustrated in the episode of a young mother who attended a grief session after her teenage daughter was killed in an auto accident. There a professional counselor waxed eloquent about what *not* to say. "One thing I can't stand," he said, "is for people to come up, touch my hand, and say, 'You have my sympathy,' or simply 'my condolences.' " This, of course, is exactly what a lot of people do say because they don't know what else to say.

The young, grief-stricken mother raised her hand and said, "I don't feel quite that way about it. When my daughter was killed by a drunken driver, there were some who came to me and said those very things. I felt for them. They were trying their best. It was a difficult situation. And maybe the words they used were clichés, but at least they were doing what they could." She went on to say, "My neighbor was totally devastated. He came over and said absolutely all the wrong things, but I knew he cared. He did what he could."

Why is it so hard to know what to say? It usually is not because people are insensitive. In fact, they probably are overly sensitive. They are afraid they may say something that would cause the hurting person to feel even worse.

Two of the major factors involved in most tragedies are failure and mystery, and many people have difficulty dealing with both. Since we have a tendency to be success-oriented and are attuned to winning, dealing with any kind of failure is difficult. To be sure, the people involved may not be responsible for the failure, but nevertheless, we find it perplexing to know what to say at a time of failure.

No matter what circumstances may have brought about a divorce, the marriage was a failure. That does not mean that the people themselves were failures, a thought that is important as the two try to rebuild their lives, but the marriage did break up.

While the simple knowledge that we often stand mute in the presence of failure does not put words in our mouths, it does define part of our problem and give us a beginning point to learn to cope with it.

The other area we are ill-equipped to deal with is mystery. Why is a young expectant mother at the dawn of an ascending career suddenly turned into a quadriplegic? Why does the IQ of a brilliant writer go from 135 to less than 100 in a year because of Alzheimer's disease? We don't have answers to such questions, and we generally are uncomfortable with questions to which we don't have answers. Can we accept the fact that we are finite and that as such we will always have to deal with a certain amount of mystery in life? Can we perhaps even grow as we ponder some of the mysteries of life? (Chapter 6 will deal more with mystery.)

I suggested at the beginning of this chapter that people sometimes begin with theory and then put that theory into practice in actual situations. At other times the reverse is true. By "getting our feet wet" and learning by experience, both good and bad, we develop a theory.

A few brief situations were described in this first chapter, with suggestions for what one might say in given circumstances. The next chapter presents the theory behind some of the practical suggestions that were made. Theory and practice can affirm each other.

2

Getting in Tune with Life

The skill of knowing what to say is not an instrument that can be picked up when needed and then laid aside. It must become a part of life, and life is a combination of a number of factors and experiences. In musicians' terminology, a musical composition is a combination of melody, rhythm, harmony, and meter. At times life is simple, and at other times it is complex as various forces and experiences counter each other. Getting in tune with life, then, calls for an examination of its various rhythms and harmonies. Let's examine four basic principles that can help us as we search for the right words to say.

1. *Life comes to us as a whole, a mixture of joy and sorrow.* Long ago the writer of Ecclesiastes taught that life comes to us as a mixture. He said it so well that his message has been repeated often, even in song:

> There is a time for everything,
>> and a season for every activity under heaven:
>>> a time to be born and a time to die,
>>> a time to plant and a time to uproot,

> a time to kill and a time to heal,
> a time to tear down and a time to build,
> a time to weep and a time to laugh,
> a time to mourn and a time to dance,
> a time to scatter stones and a time to gather them,
> a time to embrace and a time to refrain,
> a time to search and a time to give up,
> a time to keep and a time to throw away,
> a time to tear and a time to mend,
> a time to be silent and a time to speak,
> a time to love and a time to hate,
> a time for war and a time for peace.

(3:1-8)

Not all of these times are equally enjoyable, but they are part of life as a whole, a mixture of joy and sorrow. In that way they are equally natural. We may not like all of them, but we adjust to them.

Children begin to learn about this mixture at an early age. They experience joy and pain. Romping on Grandpa's knee makes them laugh. Touching a hot stove brings tears. The death of a pet is deep tragedy. It is also an opportunity to develop understanding of life's greater tragedies, although children may not be able to imagine anything more sorrowful than the loss of a pet. In retrospect, as adults, the death of a pet is a relatively minor event in the span of life. But even minor events can help us get in tune with our lives.

Essentially death is a loss. It may be a healthy exercise for us to reflect on a variety of losses, some little and some big. It is important to remember, however, that what may be a small loss to one person may be a great loss to someone else. We need to develop a sensitivity to other people's losses so that we do not judge them to be minor or insignificant because they may seem that way to us. In a sense, the loss of a pet, a toy, a friend, a job, the ability to do something, sight, hearing, or the use of an arm or a leg are all "deaths."

We all experience losses, and learning to adapt to a new situation in the aftermath helps us to get in tune with how life often is. Simply knowing that losses happen is not going to take away the pain of the next loss. Nor is the mouthing of this truth an effective way to bring comfort to a person at a time of tragedy, certainly not if that is the first thing we say. Nevertheless, having that knowledge in reserve provides resources for conversation at the appropriate time in the grief process.

If we are insensitive to people who go through what to us seem to be little losses, it is not likely that all at once we will have the skill of knowing what to say when the ultimate loss of death comes. For life comes as a whole, a mixture of joy and sorrow, and the more sensitive we are to all of life, the more sensitive we will be at a time of great tragedy.

2. *Life has different meanings for different people.* Getting in tune with life means recognizing that life has different meanings for different people. Knowing what to say to a person when tragedy strikes that person's family means first of all recognizing what his or her view of life may be.

Some of us have a deeply religious view of life, but some others do not. Because we want others to have the same comfort and joy that we have experienced in times of trial, we may attempt to impose our beliefs on them. It is appropriate to share our faith with others at some point in life, but it need not be the first thing that comes from our mouths at the time of tragedy. We need to begin where the hurting person is, and each person is at a different place. That is another way of saying that we need to begin by listening. Tragedy is not the time to convert others to our religious beliefs. I am not saying that all religious beliefs are of equal value, but I am saying that the first moments of tragedy are hardly the appropriate time to pit one religious belief against another.

An attitude of tolerance stands one in good stead. Tolerance cannot be turned off and on at will. If you generally are tolerant of other people's viewpoints, that characteristic will display itself in your first comments to a person who has just experienced the death of a friend or family member.

Even people with a deep religious faith who are very much at home with favorite verses of comfort from the Bible may not at all be in a mood to have Scripture quoted to them immediately after the death of a loved one. They may be angry, and they ought to be allowed to be angry. At a later time they may indeed want someone to share meaningful Scripture passages with them, but for the time being they may see life and death from a totally different perspective than we do. We need to allow them to be themselves at that vulnerable time.

Recognizing that people are different and that these differences need to be respected, particularly during the stress of a tragedy, is another way of getting in tune with life.

3. *Life is filled with new beginnings.* Saying that life is filled with new beginnings should not be our first words to someone who has just experienced a loss of any kind—death, divorce, or a prison term. But it is a fact of life, and sooner or later it will be the message of hope.

It is a message of hope also for those of us who, even with our best intentions, still botched up the situation when we went to bring comfort to someone in the very early moments of bereavement or tragedy. The truth is that these situations are difficult, and usually we don't know what to say. When we do say something, and it comes out all wrong, we feel like we have been utter failures. There is a new beginning for us the next time we face a similar situation. The very fact that we tried is what will be remembered. It is not so much what we say that will make an impression but the fact that we were there. So let's not berate ourselves if we feel we have said the wrong thing.

4. *Life rewards the helper with help.* In helping others we are helped. Knud Knudsen, a prominent German sculptor, expressed the thought well in a bronze sculpture titled *Koinonia* ("Community"). The sculpture depicts a side view of three characters, arms interlocked, all in forward motion, seemingly pulling a heavy load. The character pulling in front is tall, strong, and almost erect, obviously providing the major strength for the task. Those with religious inclinations will quickly identify this figure as Jesus.

The rear figure is in an almost kneeling position. The sculptor skillfully portrays the weight of this person's burden, even though the burden itself is not visually present.

Between these two figures is a third person, not as erect as the first nor as bent over as the other. The one in the center is the helper, the one for whom this book is written. But in the process of helping, he himself is being helped by the "strong one" ahead of him and by the person he is helping.

This truth is often the strong motivating factor in encouraging us to be sensitive to people going through a tragedy and being supportive of them. It happens over and over again: we go to cheer up someone who has a terminal illness, and we in turn receive strength from him or her.

Knud Knudsen's sculpture is a reminder to us that we are not alone when we reach out our hands to someone in tragedy. Whatever inner strength we have—and it may be weak indeed—is bolstered by help from a greater strength, to say nothing of the strength that comes in a deep personal interaction with the one we are trying to help.

So the purpose of this book is not to give you all the answers, for no one has them all. Rather it is to give you confidence to make a beginning.

The remaining chapters cover what to say when dealing with people in specific circumstances such as death, terminal illness, and divorce.

3

What to Say at the Time of a Death

Talking to Children About Death

The Haroldsons and Edmunds had spent New Year's Eve together for years. One New Year's Eve they were at the Edmunds' when midway through the evening word came that Grandma Edmund had died in Seattle. Grandma had been particularly close to eight-year-old Andy and ten-year-old Paul Edmund. Her death was unexpected, so the family was in a state of shock.

Dick and Fran Haroldson told the Edmunds, "We'll do whatever you like. If you would rather be alone, we'll go home. Or, if you would feel better if we stayed, we'd be glad to stay."

The Edmunds talked it over and decided that Grandma would have wanted them to continue with the evening, so the Haroldsons stayed, although the evening's festivities continued on a lower key. Even now, a number of years later, Andy and Paul Edmund remember what Dick Haroldson said to them.

He sat down between the two boys and encouraged them to tell him about their grandmother. "What was she like?" he asked. "What are some of the fun things you remember about her?" Dick didn't have to do much talking at all. His main functions were to encourage Andy and Paul to talk and then to listen to them.

Talking to children about the death of someone close to them, such as a parent, grandparent, or playmate, is a difficult task. You may be tempted to think that you don't need to take talking to children too seriously. However, children should not be treated as second-class people whom one can easily afford to ignore, for they understand far more than one may think.

Ignoring grieving children is a cop-out used by some adults because it is more difficult to talk to children about death than to adults. On the other hand, talking to hurting children can be a challenge to get down to basics, not to get children to understand—which even adults cannot do—but to be introduced to some profound mysteries that are apprehended purely by experience.

What should one say to a five- or six-year-old child? Here is one attempt: "We've got some very sad news to tell you. Grandpa just died. That means we won't see him again. Oh, we'll see him a couple of times yet. He'll be in a casket, and he'll look like he's sleeping, but he won't come back to live with us anymore."

The child very likely will say, "Why did he die?" Your answer will depend on the circumstances. If he had a long illness, you might say, "You know, we're all going to have to die sometime. Grandpa was sick for a long time. His body was wearing out. It's kind of like your old wagon; it finally just wore out. Our bodies are like that, too." Or "Do you remember when your pet parakeet died? Grandpa's dying is something like that. It makes us sad. But then we remember the good times we had with him, just like you remember the fun you had with your parakeet."

A different approach could be used if the death was sudden or if a parent or someone much younger than Grandpa had died. Here there is an even greater emphasis on mystery. "Jason, we don't know why these things happen, but they do. We all are going to die sometime, but some people die earlier than others. We love you very much, and [the person who died] loved you very much. We're going to miss him [her] very much. He [she] didn't want to die either."

Children understand the emotion of sadness. They undoubtedly have experienced it before, whenever they had a loss, whether of a toy or a pet. Allow children to feel sad. Sadness is an acceptable emotion.

It may be more difficult to talk to a grieving child who is not a member of your family. Here the temptation to ignore the child may be even greater. When you go to the home or mortuary to visit with the adults in the family of survivors, don't pass by the challenge of also showing an interest in the children. A beginning conversation might be, "Jason, I'm so sorry to hear that your [_____] died. I loved him [her] very much, and I'm sure you did, too. I bet you are sad, aren't you? What are some of the good things you remember about him [her]?" Here again is that fundamental guideline: Be a listener. Make it as easy as possible for the person you are trying to console to feel comfortable in saying what he or she wants to say.

Some of your comments will be determined by the religious background of the family. If both you and the family are devoutly religious and you know them well, you will undoubtedly want to make some reference to spiritual values and eternity. But exercise care not to speak too glibly about religious faith. It may sound very nice to you to say, "God wanted to give her a nice place in heaven" or "She is with Jesus now," but a child may well reason, "I need her more than God does." One 40-year-old man is still angry at angels. He bears emotional scars from when, as a six-year-old, he was told that angels came and took his father to heaven. The question of how much to say of spiritual matters is dealt with at greater length in chapter 8.

Research shows that the greatest fear that children have when there is a death in the family is that they will be left alone. Conversation with young children, therefore, should emphasize as much as possible that they are part of the family and will not be forsaken. Children also have fear at times that they caused a death or a divorce. They think the world revolves around themselves, and they attribute great power to themselves. Often they don't voice this fear, but they harbor it. Adults can help children put this fear to rest and relieve guilt by indicating that the situation was caused by other factors.

Talking About the Death of a Young Person

The death of children may be the most difficult to deal with. I personally went through that experience not long ago. My daughter and son-in-law adopted a Taiwanese boy. The process was a long one, and so the eagerness of seeing the child for the first time was overwhelming. What a joy it was finally to be at the Minneapolis airport not only to see the six-month-old baby for the first time but also to observe the indescribable thrill of the parents as they held their child for the first time.

Sixteen days later the parents and the baby were guests at the home of the couple who were to be godparents at the baptism, which was planned for the Sunday after Easter. The child played on the floor. Then the parents gave him a bottle and he went to sleep. Meanwhile the adults went into the dining room to eat. When they came back to pick up the baby, he was dead. An undetected viral infection for which he had no immunity had killed him.

The funeral was held at the college where the parents were on the staff, and the president of the college preached the sermon. At the funeral home on the evening before the funeral, another faculty couple, who had lost an infant twenty years earlier, said, "It's still painful. You never really forget it."

The first question my wife and I had was not about the philosophical or theological issues of why this child died. Rather our immediate question was, "What do we say?" We pondered this as we drove the 150 miles to be with our daughter and son-in-law. The question was rather easily answered: we didn't say anything. For a long time we all just held each other tight. Then, when words began to come, they came rather naturally. Again, the value of the guideline that says, "Make it as easy as possible for the person to whom you are talking to say what he or she wants to say," was borne out. The most likely thing the hurting person will want to tell is how the death happened.

But what do you say to grieving persons if you don't have a close enough relationship to hug them? In times of grief it becomes easy to touch. A mere handshake becomes more than a handshake; it becomes a long holding and stroking. Probably at no other time is the sense of touch so meaningful. Eventually words will come, and even if they are somewhat awkward and your later reflection on them embarrasses you, be assured that the touch was the most important.

The more sudden the death and the younger the person who died, the more difficult it seems to know what to say. There are times when you shouldn't say anything, at least not for a time, and then perhaps very little. You just ponder the mystery, and the hand on the shoulder and the touch on the arm communicate that both the consoler and the one being consoled are involved in an experience so deep that they understand each other even though little is said. Strength has flowed from one to the other, and it has not been in only one direction. Both have been strengthened.

The difficulty in finding words at the moment is also a reminder that the obligation may be deeper than simply having something to say at the time. If you truly care—and, of course, this will depend somewhat on the relationship you have with the person—you will want to commit yourself to an extended showing of concern.

Showing Care Before and After the Funeral

There are at least three crucial times of need for a family that has experienced a death. One is immediate. That is when we wonder, "What do I say?" Some things you say may be better than others; some may be downright improper; and you may well kick yourself all the way home for having said something stupid.

When people are going through tragedy, they are at their most vulnerable, and comments often make a greater impact than under ordinary circumstances. Words are often remembered and quoted for many years, with praise heaped on the person who left a positive impression and disgust retained for the one who said the "wrong thing."

At a later time you may have opportunity to express regret for what you said, and if so, fine. But don't count on it, because sometimes when trying to undo something, you just dig yourself in deeper. You don't need to live with guilt because you tried and failed. It is time for a new beginning.

Several weeks after the funeral is another crucial time of need for a family. By this time the numbness has worn off. The emptiness of the home now becomes depressing. Reality strikes hard as one realizes that the loved one will not be coming back. Gradually one has to come to terms with that fact. And it's painful.

By now all of the casseroles and dishes that friends and neighbors brought over between the death and the funeral are gone. Now is the opportunity for another expression of care giving. Now is the time to call again, either on the telephone or in person, and say, "How are things going?" Some have found it helpful to call their grieving friend once a day and talk only a minute or so. This practice of "touching base" gives the one receiving the calls both a reassurance that someone cares and an opportunity to get into deeper issues when the time is right.

Invite a newly widowed friend over to your home for a meal or suggest that you go out for lunch or dinner. Again remember the guideline, "Make it as easy as possible for the one who has suffered the loss to say whatever he or she would like to say." Most likely you will have no difficulty making conversation. Don't avoid all reference to the death as though it hadn't happened. Make it comfortable to talk about.

Above all, keep including newly widowed people in your social activities. Our culture is so couples oriented that we have difficulty knowing what to do with odd numbers. Tables are set for four, six, eight, ten, or twelve. One widow told of her experience in being excluded, virtually immediately, from former get-togethers:

We were part of a bridge club and played bridge rather regularly, but as soon as John died, I was no longer invited to bridge parties. I know that you need couples and even numbers for bridge games, and I know also that some people would be hesitant to invite a single woman and a single man for fear this would be interpreted as match-making. My guess is, however, that there are probably a number of widows and widowers or other single people around, and what would be so wrong with achieving an even number, made up of eight women and four men or vice versa or five of one gender and seven of another?

Be hesitant in deciding that it is time for someone to be through with the grief process. People have different time frames in responding to grief, and their friends should not be too quick in setting someone else's grieving schedule, without at least having tried a more positive approach, such as inviting and including the grieving person in some of their own activities.

Anniversaries or the first holidays after a death are a third crucial time of need. If a family has always gone together to a Christmas Eve candlelight service or to an Easter service or to an annual concert, the first time they go without one member of the family—particularly a spouse—can be a sad or even traumatic experience. This is a time for friends to be sensitive and to show some kind of support.

This support could be in the form of a card with a note attached: "This must be a particularly difficult time for you. I just want you to know that I am thinking about you." Anniversaries of weddings or special events or the death bring back memories. It helps to have others remember the occasion in the absence of the one who is no longer there.

There are all kinds of ways that one can be supportive to people even though they may not be acquainted with each other. One man makes it a point of watching the newspaper and noting any death that has occurred as a result of a gun accident. His own son was killed in such an accident. When he sees a story of a similar incident in the paper, he drops a note to the family of the victim even though they may be strangers to him. Common sorrow and grief can become the basis for developing a strong friendship.

Exercising Tough Love

There may come a time when you have to exercise tough love. Another person may become so preoccupied with his or her problem and grief that it gets out of hand. At such a point it is acceptable to say to a person, "I know you are going through some very difficult times, but I am somewhat concerned about you. Do you want to share some of your feelings with several of us? You don't have to bear this alone." Many hospitals and other health organizations have support groups for grieving persons. Testimonials from people who have attended such groups bear witness to their effectiveness.

In the following chapters we will discuss how to talk with those who have experienced other kinds of losses— the loss of health and the loss of a spouse.

4

What to Say to Someone Who Is Terminally Ill

You remember Jane and Carol from the introduction. It took Jane eight years to feel free to talk with Carol about the accident that had made her a quadriplegic. During those eight years something else happened to Jane that dramatically changed her life—another close friend of hers, Julie, died of cancer.

"I'll never be the same again," said Jane. "Julie taught me all about death, and in so doing, she also taught me a lot about life. Had I had my experience with Julie before Carol's accident, I would have been a little better prepared to have known what to say to Carol."

Julie had been visiting her brother and sister when she became ill. The doctor diagnosed it as diverticulitis, but the usual remedies did not seem to work. Further examination indicated malignancy, and ten months later she died.

But Julie took complete charge of her death and involved seven other carefully chosen people in the last months of her life. She had known each of them for a

number of years: her college roommate and her husband; a widow who was a coworker, the oldest of the
group; another woman coworker; a man who was a
former coworker; a woman who had been a friend for
years; and Jane, the youngest of the group.

Jane had driven Julie to the clinic for her chemo-
therapy, and they had joked about her hair falling out.

"Our relationship was always upbeat," said Jane. "It
had been that way all of our lives. Maybe that's why it
was so important that I be one of those in the inner
circle during her last days."

About six weeks before she died, Julie called her seven
friends to her hospital bed and told them, "It doesn't
look like I'm going to make it. I have three choices: I
can die here in the hospital, I can go to the hospice, or
I can go home to my apartment and die there. I have
made my decision, and I'm sort of interested in what
you think. Since I will have round-the-clock nursing
wherever I am, I'd like to go to my apartment."

"We all approved," Jane said. "We promised that one
of us would look in on her every day and that she would
die in the arms of one of us."

Julie didn't fear death, but she was angry about dying.
She was frustrated about the many things she would
have liked to accomplish. According to some definitions,
Julie was not a particularly religious person, at least not
the kind who talked about her religion a lot. She went
to church, but there were some Sunday mornings when
she could be found in her sailboat rather than in a
church pew.

But Julie had a deep faith, and in the last few months
of her life that faith gave strength not only to her but
to her seven friends as well. Her house was filled with
plants, symbols of life, and one time when Jane visited
her, Julie said, "Hear the birds outside. I was hoping I

would live until spring so I could hear the birds sing once more." They sat and listened, cried a little and laughed a little, and remembered their earlier days when they had gone sailing together.

"One thing I want you to promise me," Julie said to Jane, "and that is that you will take sailing lessons so you can become a better sailor; you can use some improvement."

"Oh, I will," Jane promised, "and every time I'm out there on the boat, I know you'll be keeping an eye on me."

Later Jane learned that Julie had willed her sailboat to her.

"Humor was so much a part of our relationship," Jane said, "and yet we weren't playing any games. We knew what the situation was, and we could talk about it. We cried and told each other how much we meant to each other."

During her last week Julie was in a coma much of the time. About 36 hours before she died, she suddenly became very lucid at seven o'clock in the morning. She asked her nurse to call all of her friends. All seven of them came in a matter of hours. She talked with each of them individually for about five minutes. She asked Jane and one of the other women to sing at her funeral, the same number they had sung at Julie's mother's funeral. The next day Julie died in the arms of her former college roommate.

The funeral was on April 1. "Just like Julie," her friends said. "She would have planned it that way. She had the last laugh on death."

It would be wrong to say that it was easy to talk to Julie during her terminal illness. Something like that is never easy. But at least her attitude was such that there was an openness to talk about her illness. She knew she was about to die; her friends knew it, and each knew that all the others knew it. That made it easier for everyone to deal with the terminal illness.

Getting the Right Perspective

While there is no one way to talk with everyone who is terminally ill—each circumstance is different—Jane's sharing of her last few weeks with Julie does provide some insights into the question, "What do you say to someone who is terminally ill?"

In a sense, of course, we all are terminally ill, but that is *not* the thing to say on your first learning of a friend's terminal illness. Nevertheless, it is helpful to remind ourselves that death will come to all.

The prime of life, too, can be a relative thing. One doctor, in brief remission from cancer but fully aware of what his future was, talked to an adult Sunday school class about his impending death. He was in his early fifties, and someone had remarked about the tragedy of being taken in the prime of life.

"Who is to say what the prime of life is?" he asked. "For some people it may be at the age of two, for others at 16, for others at 50, and for still others at 75."

Again this is not the sort of thing you would say to a terminally ill person, at least not during the early stages, but it is a good philosophy to keep in mind.

Perhaps the most helpful insight in knowing what to say is to be aware of timing. Do not answer questions too quickly. Again the cardinal rule holds, "Make it as easy as possible for the ill person to say what he or she wants to say."

It is quite possible to be caught in a moment of embarrassment, for both persons are wondering what the other is thinking and how much the other knows about the actual situation. Neither is sure if the other person wants to talk about it.

Often a question is the best way to break the ice. "How do you feel?" is at least a beginning. Other questions might be "What is your situation?" or "How ill are you, Peter?" The response to those questions may also give clues about how much the person knows about his or her condition and how much he or she wants to talk about the illness.

Of course, there cannot always be a total certainty that the illness is indeed terminal, so there needs to be a balance between hope and reality. No purpose is served by holding out false hope, but neither should every word be shrouded in gloom.

It is important not only to understand that a person may be angry but also to tolerate that anger. If he or she is at all religiously inclined, comfort may come from the fact that some Psalm writers were quite vehement in expressing anger. This anger was often expressed against other people (Psalms 58, 109) but sometimes in laments against God and the seeming delay in answers to prayers (Psalms 22, 60).

In Psalm 44, for instance, the writer wondered why the Lord rejected his people in spite of their faithfulness.

> Awake, O Lord! Why do you sleep?
> > Rouse yourself! Do not reject us forever.
> > Why do you hide your face
> > > and forget our misery and oppression?
> > > > (vv. 23-24)

It is perfectly normal and acceptable for good relig-ious people to be angry. It is helpful to note, however, that each of these Psalms also has notes of high confidence. Anger against tragedy and strength to bear the tragedy are two sides of the same coin.

Again the words of Ecclesiastes come to mind:

> A time to weep and a time to laugh,
> a time to mourn and a time to dance,
> ....
> a time to be silent and a time to speak.
>
> (3:4, 7b)

Relating to the Terminally Ill

Two friends, Karen and Marianne, sat side by side at a concert. Marianne had inoperable cancer, and everyone knew it.

"How are you?" Karen asked, smiling.

"O fine," Marianne replied, also smiling. There was a slight pause, and then Marianne turned to Karen. "Were you just asking that, or do you really want to know?"

They both recognized that they had been caught in a cultural trap, saying what was expected. Of course, we do ask people how they are, even though often we do not even wait for the answer or fail to pay attention to it. We reply, "Fine," whether we really are or not. But Marianne was not taking life for granted anymore. And Karen indeed had been interested in finding out how Marianne was, even though the question may have been phrased as a cliché.

It was a rich experience as Marianne shared her feelings and how she and her whole family were preparing for her death.

But unsurprisingly that depth of conversation seldom just happens, for terminal illness does not lend itself to easy conversation.

So what do you say? It would be useless to have memorized lines appropriate for all occasions, for each situation is different. At the risk of appearing to give simple answers that can be repeated in what seem to be similar experiences, here is a suggested conversation that may give some ideas for adaptation.

Jean, a thirty-five-year-old mother with two small children, has just had exploratory surgery and has been told that she has inoperable cancer that has already invaded her liver. She is now in the room alone as you come in to visit her. She is crying, and she is angry. What do you say?

Before you say anything, touch her, probably her hand. Don't feel that you have to say something right away, even if the next five seconds seem to be five minutes. Above all, don't interrupt her if she is saying something or seems to be wanting to say something.

"How are you feeling?" is a perfectly normal thing to say, and it can be asked in a way that indicates that you really are interested in knowing. Chances are that you will need to say very little except to affirm the person.

To say, "Everything's going to be all right," is not very helpful. The patient knows better. She may be angry. She may sob. No good purpose is served in trying to get her to stop crying. Your major function is *just to be there* and perhaps to cry with her.

At the end of the visit, you may want to say, "Jean, I'm truly sorry to hear this news. I wish I knew what to say. I love you. Maybe tomorrow we can talk about it some more. I'll be glad to stay if you want me to. Or if you'd rather be alone for a while, I'll come back tomorrow or this evening. Is there anything at all that I can do for you or bring you?"

Understanding the Stages of Terminal Illness

It is important to remember that this book was written not to comfort the ill person but to make communication easier for the person who is wondering what to say. If it were written for the terminally ill person, it would review and elaborate on the various stages of accepting terminal illness and death as described by Elisabeth Kübler-Ross: denial, anger, bargaining, depression, and acceptance (*On Death and Dying* [New York: Macmillan, 1970]).

Nor is this book intended to make a professional counselor out of the one who reads it. But, even so, it is helpful to be somewhat familiar with at least a few of Kübler-Ross's stages, for one would say different things to a person who is in the denial or anger stage than to one who has reached the stage of acceptance.

At least for the time being, allow the ill person to be in the stage in which he or she is. If she is angry, let her be angry. Your main function at this point may be simply to listen, not to tell her what to think or to contradict her. It may be a bit risky, but this may even be the time for a little humor, for humor can sometimes be the best antidote to anger. In fact, be angry along with her: "Yeah, this is unfair. You shouldn't take this lying down." Both of you may suddenly become aware of the pun and break out laughing.

You may be caught in a particularly difficult situation if the person is in the denial stage. On one hand, you should not agree with her and say, "Of course, you're going to snap out of this. Everything is going to be fine." On the other hand, this is not the time to contradict her with rough or even mild statements of reality: "Quit kidding yourself. You know you're going to die." The ill person will come to that conclusion soon enough when she gets to another stage. Leave it to a professional counselor to help her through the denial stage. As an "amateur" but as a friend who at least wants to say something, let it be a comment along these lines: "The doctors will undoubtedly want to do some more tests, and let's hope that some new kind of medication can be found."

The deepest level is when the ill person finally accepts that she is going to die. At this point the conversation can often become most meaningful. Since conversation implies both speaking and listening, you as the consoler should be prepared to do more listening than speaking. That does not mean you should always just sit there quietly; take your cue from what the ill person is saying.

Above all, don't correct the ill person in the stage of acceptance by saying, "Oh, you're going to be all right. You'll be up and around in no time."

In Knud Knudsen's sculpture, mentioned in chapter 2, the helper is helped. As the consoler trying to bring strength to the sick person, you may gain incredible strength for yourself. In this final stage of acceptance, the sick person may well have a renewed insight and sense of values that will enrich your own life. Listen carefully.

Now is also a time to be aware of some basic courtesies. The sick person may be tired or weak yet be too gracious to tell you that. Don't insist on talking. Neither feel that just by being there you are doing nothing. Your presence can be a comfort in itself. Some researchers say that the one thing feared most by those about to die is being left alone. Even though they may no longer be able to talk and may be in a coma, they can sense your presence. Some few may want to be alone. Play it by ear. Trust your good judgment whether it is best to be in the room or to leave.

Your decision whether to stay as the time of death approaches will depend in part on your relationship to the sick person. Members of the immediate family will, of course, want to remain close. Unless you are a very close friend, you will have said your good-bye at an earlier time and will not intrude on the family at this time.

Talking to Those Who Are "Mildly" Ill

There is another category of illness in which it may not be as stressfully difficult to know what to say but is nevertheless awkward: "mild" sickness, if indeed there is such a thing.

Let's say a friend is spending some time at a hospital. It may be for a test or for routine surgery. While doctors say that all surgery has some risk connected with it, no one is greatly concerned that this surgery will be serious.

However, a couple days of hospitalization is required, and you want to visit the patient. What do you say? In all probability the conversation will be light-hearted. There will be some joking, and the conversation will virtually take care of itself.

At the same time, it would be wise at least to be alert to some possible signs of anxiety. Obviously the visitor should not instill unnecessary fear in the mind of the patient. The question How are you feeling? is always in order. It will put the ball in the court of the patient, and he or she will supply information. Don't pry, but show genuine interest in the patient. The information will likely be both verbal and nonverbal, spoken words and mannerisms accompanying the words.

Don't try to become an amateur psychologist, ana-lyzing your friend's every comment and action, but remain sensitive to his or her feelings. Enjoy the visit. Your presence is more important than what you are likely to say. If your friend is in pain or would rather be alone, you can sense that and should keep your visit short. But even then you will have indicated your interest and your visit will be remembered.

A rather typical attitude is that we always have to be upbeat. We are told, "Don't be negative; be positive about everything." We often view sadness as a bad emotion. We may feel that we always have to cheer everybody up. Visiting someone who is ill may well put us back in touch with some of the positive feelings associated with sadness. It helps bind us together. That does not mean that we have to go out of our way to make the visit a sad one, but neither should we be afraid of using the occasion to share sadness.

Each time you visit an ill person you will find yourself growing and becoming more comfortable with finding the right words to say.

While illness is indeed a part of life, it is not a part of the essence of life. It may bring an end to life as we know it, but it also opens the door to a consideration of the mystery beyond life, a mystery that is its own reward.

5

What to Say When Friends Get Divorced

The fact that divorce is much more common today than it was in the past does not make it any less painful to talk about. And while the stigma that it still carries in some circles probably will never totally disappear, an attempt is being made to be more sensitive to the pain that people experience in a divorce. Both people in a divorce face major life-style changes that lead to a time of grieving. Even the one who initiated the divorce might express relief outwardly but have painful, unexpressed inner feelings that almost tear him or her apart.

The paradox is that deeply religious people who have been trained to be kind, considerate, and caring sometimes have the greatest difficulty in showing that kindness to people who are being or have been divorced. This insensitivity shows itself not in making unkind and cutting remarks but in saying nothing, very likely not because they really are insensitive but because they just do not know what to say.

One divorced wife tells her story. For many years she and her husband had been missionaries in Africa during the days when the prevalent missionary policy was that unless a woman missionary was single and called to serve a specific task, such as being a nurse, teacher, secretary, or some other traditionally female occupation, she was not salaried.

When male missionaries were called, their wives were expected to do whatever had to be done without pay. Church mission board policy has changed considerably since then, but there were a number of family casualties during the earlier policy.

This particular couple reached an amiable agreement to divorce, but it was not without considerable pain. On the night the decision was made, the wife wrote a letter to 25 close friends, most of whom were active church members. She said:

> I just wanted you to get this information directly from me and not second-hand. Frank and I are getting a divorce. It is not necessary to go into all of the reasons and incidents that led to this decision. It has been a painful experience, and we are not blaming each other. Above all, I don't want you to blame Frank. We hope you will continue to be friends with both of us. After tomorrow, my address will be _____, and Frank will live at _____.

She had expected that she might get a card or letter from several of her friends to acknowledge the letter and perhaps even give a word of support and affirmation. But from the 25 persons to whom she wrote the letter, she received only one response, and that was from a person who considered herself an agnostic.

As in many other painful situations, we do not have enough experience with what our friends are going through in a divorce to be able to respond very well. Perhaps if we understand why divorces are more prevalent today, we will be less judgmental. Any form of judgmental behavior, no matter how covert, will hinder communication.

In an earlier day when divorce was less common, living with unhappiness and perhaps even abuse was considered the lesser of two evils. And some people who go through divorce today may agree that, all things considered, they may be worse off after the divorce than before. It is also likely that some couples going through divorce could have done some things to avoid that serious step. But for many couples, for many reasons, divorce was the lesser of two evils.

Different values and expectations have certainly had an effect on the divorce rate. Years ago people were accustomed to having one member of the household set values for all. This led to outward agreement. Cultural pressures were directed toward conformity. In contrast, today many people do not suppress their preferences and values, and our culture presents us with a complex variety of possibilities. Diversity is encouraged. Social pressures have lessened for couples to stay together no matter how toxic a marriage has become.

Another factor that is hard on marriages is the expectation for a high standard of living with an increasing variety of material possessions and comforts. For many couples expenses get so high that two incomes are required, so both husband and wife work. Both might come home tired at night. Children might get on their nerves. While some people can somehow balance all of these activities and perhaps even thrive on them, for others the string simply becomes too taut and breaks.

The reason for devoting space here to the causes of divorce is to help us be more sensitive and empathetic.

This is not the time to judge them, abandon them, or encourage guilt. This is the time they really need your help and understanding.

Knowing what to say is not easy. Each situation will be different, of course, and your comments will depend on your relationship with the couple and in what stage the couple is when you find out about the divorce. Here are some possible situations.

1. *When you first begin to pick up clues that there may be some problems.* Sometimes there are such clues. The husband and wife are rarely seen together or seem to do fewer and fewer things as a couple.

It may be that one or the other has dropped comments from time to time that they are having problems. Since everybody has problems, you may have thought this was just natural when in fact it may have been a mild call for help.

All at once you see a pattern forming and you think that there may be a problem. Depending on how well you know the couple, you might say to one of them, "Jack [or Susan], I have gotten the feeling recently that you and Susan [or Jack] are having problems. I don't want to pry or butt in, and if I'm wrong, please do forgive me and I won't mention it again, but if there is a problem and you want to share it with me, I have open ears and a closed mouth."

Taking this step certainly involves risk. It may even cost you a friendship, although that is not likely if you have approached the question with sensitivity. If your friend assures you that absolutely nothing is wrong, then you can drop the matter. If, however, there is some substance to what you say, then you at least will have provided an opportunity for your friend to share, an opportunity for which your friend will be grateful.

Now some of the major guidelines immediately come into play. Make it as comfortable for your friend to say what he or she wants to say. Don't give advice immediately. Your major task is to listen and remain as neutral as you can. Don't immediately agree that all the fault lies in your friend's spouse.

Nurturing comments such as "It must be painful" and "Can I help in any way?" are in order. If your friend asks you to keep the matter confidential, by all means do so. You will very likely have other opportunities to talk with your friend, and in the meantime you can think over ways to be most sensitive and helpful.

2. *When you are surprised by Betty's news that she and Jeff are getting a divorce.* You have always thought they had a good marriage, so it is difficult to hide your surprise, and it is best not to try. Since she and Jeff have given the appearance of being a happy couple, it is quite in order to say, "Betty, I am surprised. I had no idea that you were having problems. I'm sorry to hear this is happening."

Then Betty will very likely say, "Your surprise is quite understandable. Jeff and I have put up a pretty good front."

Listening is more important than talking even though you obviously have to say something. Assure Betty that you will try not to pry but that you will be glad to provide a listening ear or a shoulder to cry on if that seems to be needed. Be aware that you will be hearing only one side of the story, and while it may be quite factual, there very likely is another side. Of course you won't say that to Betty. She may say it herself, and if she does, that will make your part of the conversation easier. Remember, you are not a professional counselor. It is quite in order to ask if Betty and Jeff have seen a counselor together or individually, and even to suggest that they do. A counselor's insight and support can help her through this difficult time. It may be that Betty will look to you for further opportunity to talk, but the purpose of the above suggestions for conversation merely has been to deal with the surprise with some degree of comfort.

3. *When it has become common knowledge that Kay and Andy are getting a divorce, and you run into Kay for the first time since you have heard.* In a sense, this may be the most difficult of all or at least the most embarrassing. It is much easier to say nothing, but there will come a time when you do have to say something, so it may as well be now.

So what do you say? That will depend on the circumstances and your relationship to Kay, but a good opening comment could be, "Kay, I heard that you and Andy are getting divorced. I'm sorry to hear that. There must be some pain connected with that decision, and I'm always sorry when people are in pain."

Then you may want to add, "If you prefer not to talk about it, fine. But if you want to tell me about it, I'm a good listener." You have broken the ice by letting her know that you are aware of her situation. How the conversation goes from there will depend on what Kay has to say.

4. *When the situation has reached a point where you are convinced that an intervention is necessary, even though you are not a professional counselor.* Perhaps the relationship between Barb and Mike has become so intolerable that it is obvious to all that something has to be done. There is evidence that Barb has been physically abused. Perhaps she ought to get a divorce, but she is so traumatized that decision-making is impossible. Even then you may not be the one to intervene, but Barb may be looking for someone such as you to

give signs of interest. You may begin the conversation by saying, "Barb, how are things going? You look awfully tired. Are you okay?"

In addition to the suggestions specifically appropriate for those four situations, the following thoughts may be helpful when talking to a friend who is getting a divorce.

Although listening plays a major role when talking with your friend, you may feel you need to ask some questions as well. Remember to ask him or her to clarify the situation, not from curiosity or to pry into your friend's private life.

As you talk, you may find it tempting to add to the conflict by making negative comments about his or her spouse. A better path to follow is to give brief "reflective" comments such as "That first court hearing must have been very painful," or "You didn't know getting divorced was going to be this rough, did you?"

Encourage your friend to express feelings and to keep moving on with life. He or she may benefit from joining a divorce recovery group or other personal growth group. The emotions typically experienced in divorce (regret, guilt, anger, grief, and sadness) can be so overwhelming that it often is wise for a divorcing person to see a professional counselor.

Remember that you probably know little about the factors that contributed to the divorce. Perhaps the husband had withdrawn from the marriage and didn't express his feelings, or the wife consistently spent more than their two incomes brought in, or one spouse kept growing emotionally and intellectually while the other remained immature. Be a good listener and be supportive, but do not judge.

Divorce is a major loss, and all the suggestions for helping people with their grief apply here. Some people are so devastated by divorce that their health is adversely affected or they experience long-lasting depression for which they may need professional help. The grief and pain are usually intense. Holidays and anniversaries are particularly difficult, and words of caring are in order: "I know how much Christmas means to you, but this year it might be a sad time. Could we plan to do some things together?"

The words are not as important as the message they give that you care and won't be judgmental. As in the case of death, so here also, the opportunity and obligation for long-term caring, both during the process of divorcing and after, are important. Some people who have gone through both experiences, the death of a spouse and a divorce, say that divorce is the more difficult. Death at least brings some closure and finality. Divorce often does so only in theory. The divorced spouses may continue to run into each other or need to meet on a regular basis to arrange for child care. If the experience has been a particularly bitter or painful one, memories will linger and wounds will open afresh.

An additional source of pain for divorced persons is to be ostracized by most of their friends. It may be worse just to be ignored. One woman, reflecting on the pain of her own divorce, said: "You know, at the time of a death, people send flowers or a card and come over to talk. A divorce is just as painful, and to be forgotten at that time is most painful of all."

Developing greater sensitivity in finding the right words to say to a person just divorced or going through a divorce can ease a tremendous amount of pain. Trust yourself to be able to say some words that comfort. An accepting, nonjudgmental attitude goes a long way in helping a hurting friend know that you care.

6

Nursing Homes and the Dilemma of What to Say

Having to place a family member in a nursing home or care center can be traumatic. The very fact that we talk of "placing" someone in a nursing home sounds ominous. The unspoken thought implied in "placing" is that it is against the will of the one being placed. Even under the best of circumstances, placing someone in a nursing home is always a trying experience.

There are at least three occasions related to nursing homes that raise the problem of finding the right words.

1. What do you say to someone who is in the process of deciding whether a member of the family should be placed in a nursing home?

2. What do you say to someone after a family member has been placed in a nursing home?

3. What do you say when visiting a resident in a nursing home, particularly if that person is no longer able to communicate or lives in such a fantasy world that any conversation that does take place is totally removed from reality?

Remember, we are talking about nursing homes, not retirement centers. People who move into retirement centers are still able to take care of themselves. They may be slowing down because of age and may need assistance with a few things, but essentially they are self-sufficient.

Occasionally people move into a nursing home by their own choice. They have some degree of disability and need some care or maybe even total care. Sometimes there is no close family to care for them. At other times, the family would be able to provide care in their own homes, but it would impose a severe burden; the person who needs care recognizes this and personally chooses to go to a nursing home. The rest of the family may be experiencing guilt, but the understanding attitude of the person about to go into the home eases the guilt immensely.

However, in most cases family members have to place a loved one in a nursing home because that person requires care that cannot be given at home. In fact, physicians often order that a patient be placed where he or she can receive total care. After serious struggles with various options, members often find that a nursing home is the best, if indeed not the only, solution, even though they wish it were otherwise.

1. *What do you say to someone who is in the process of deciding whether a family member should be placed in a nursing home?* The first rule in talking with families going through this struggle is to help *them* arrive at *their* decision rather than imposing your decision on them. Different people confronted with similar situations may well make different decisions.

Most of us have heard stories of tremendous faithfulness and courage of persons who take care of a spouse, parent, or child in their own home for years, denying themselves all social activity or other personal freedom. These people have their own sense of values, and for them a commitment to care personally for a member of the family no matter what the cost has top priority. This kind of commitment is all too rare in our society and should be respected.

On the other hand, some people have as their chief concern the proper care of their loved one, regardless of who does it, realizing, of course, that the family relationship may be altered if the loved one lives outside the home. They weigh the pros and cons and consider such things as how their total devotion to the care of one person will affect their relationships with others to whom they also have an obligation. This is an important consideration particularly if the mental condition of the ill person is such that he or she is unaware of who is giving the care.

No good purpose is served by reminding the people who must make the decision of whether to place a family member in a nursing home that in the "olden days" all families personally cared for their own. Nor is it helpful to drop hints that if families only had the will to help their own without resorting to a nursing home, a way could be found to work out arrangements. Such comments are insensitive and cruel.

In those "olden days," family situations usually were different. Families were larger, so there were more people to share in the caring, although even then the lot often fell to one person. Simply to say that we ought to go back to those values overlooks the fact that we live in a different world now.

The most difficult situation is when a family finds it necessary to place one of its members in a nursing home while the person is still mentally competent and perhaps even strongly opposes such placement. That is when the guilt felt by the family will be heaviest, when even after consideration of every other possibility, the circumstances seem to suggest that a nursing home is the only option.

What do you say to people who are going through this kind of struggle? It is virtually impossible to suggest specifics of conversation that might take place for such an extended conversation, but some of the basic guidelines referred to in earlier chapters hold true. Make it as easy as possible for them to say what they want to say. Don't begin by imposing your views on them. Help them think through their situation honestly. They may ask you to help them be objective, to help them determine whether they are just trying to avoid an inconvenience.

Even with the best of intentions and under the most obvious circumstances, it probably will not be possible to relieve all guilt. Both wallowing in guilt and denying guilt are counterproductive. Help the family to recognize the situation for what it is. Encourage them to talk about it as naturally as possible without being obsessed by it.

The most difficult task may be to convince the person who is being placed in the nursing home that this decision will be the best for him or her. Unless you are a family member, you probably will not be called upon to help convince the person about whom the decision is being made. If you are asked, the most helpful approach will be to assure that person both of your continuing love and of the continuing love of the family. Undoubtedly there has been every effort to find a nursing home that provides quality care, so assurance can also be given that the person will receive the assistance he or she needs.

This is also the time to rely on the skills of a professional social worker or counselor who knows how to react to the likely anger of the person whose fate is being decided.

2. *What do you say to someone after a family member has been placed in a nursing home?* There are often two extremes: to talk about it all the time or not talk about it at all, thus making it seem that the person no longer exists. Some people may not want to talk about a member of their family being in a nursing home, and you will soon discover that after a few conversations, but don't begin by assuming that is the case.

Natalie told about how friends and colleagues treated her after she had to have her husband placed in a nursing home. One day while going through the cafeteria line at the office, one of her coworkers from a different floor came up to her and said, "I've often wanted to ask how Jim is, but that must be so sad that you just don't want to talk about it. But, how is he?"

"No, as a matter of fact, I don't mind talking about it," Natalie replied. "Of course, it's sad seeing Jim who was once so brilliant and who had a delightful sense of humor so deteriorated that his IQ is probably in the sixties. But I have learned to cope. I had to accept the facts of life and make the most of it. Obviously, I wish things were not this way, but I go on living. Never talking about it but having it constantly preying on my mind makes it all the worse. Do feel free to ask about Jim anytime you wish."

Natalie told of several other experiences. Even two years after Jim was placed in a nursing home, some of her coworkers with whom she had friendly relationships still had not said one word to her about Jim. She was convinced that it was not because they were insensitive. They were probably overly sensitive and just didn't know what to say.

Every now and then Natalie would see a couple with whom she had once been closely associated. Never once did they mention anything about Jim, even though the conversation was such that it would have been very easy to ask.

Finally, when a committee meeting brought them together and they were having coffee, Natalie said, "I suppose you are wondering how Jim is."

Now the ice had been broken. They were eager to hear and, as though they had been given permission, whenever they met after this, they found it much easier to talk about Jim.

Another friend, not only of Jim and Natalie, but of their two sons as well, often visited Natalie and asked how the boys were because she had grown very fond of them. But she didn't ask about Jim anymore.

Natalie had two explanations for this reticence. She was convinced that these people were not insensitive. In fact, she sensed that they were deeply pained as they talked with her without referring to Jim. They honestly didn't know what to say. The reason it was difficult for them to know what to say, Natalie surmised, was that they thought—albeit wrongly—that it was just too painful for her to talk about.

The other reason for the reticence was far deeper. "I surmise they may think that if this could happen to a person as brilliant as Jim, then it could happen to them too, and they just can't bear the thought of that," Natalie said, "so they wipe it completely out of their minds."

Well, what do you say to a friend whose spouse or parent or child is in a nursing home? You can at least acknowledge that the friend still has a close tie to the family member in the nursing home. You can very easily ask about both. It is as simple as asking, "How is Jim these days? And how are you doing?" Simply asking how

Jim is and waiting for an answer, and perhaps following up with another question, such as "Is he in any pain?" or "Is there any change in his condition?" or "Would he welcome a visit?" will let you know whether your friend wants to talk about it some more. At least you have acknowledged the existence of a person and a relationship.

3. *What do you say when visiting a resident in a nursing home?* This may be the most difficult question of all. Perhaps the person has full mental abilities but is in physical pain or has some other debilitating condition. In that situation, there can be some kind of communication, although it still may be difficult to know what to say. Often the person feels sad about being there and may be grieving the loss of independence and good health. Too much inquiry into his or her situation may make both of you feel downhearted. After a few questions about how things are, talk about cheerful topics, recalling good times and thanking the person for his or her part in any shared memories. If the person is totally mentally incompetent, not able to talk, or in such a state of fantasy that you are at a loss for words, then wondering what to say becomes painful. Because no communication seems to be possible, you may be tempted not to visit that person at all and thus increase your guilt feelings all the more.

In situations like these, it may help to ponder the mystery. Many people are not very good at mystery. It's an attack on an all-pervasive feeling that we can do virtually anything we set our minds to doing. Give us a problem and enough time and we'll solve it. If *defeat* is in our vocabulary, it is only there temporarily. Sooner or later—and very likely, sooner—we'll come up with a solution.

Silence is another word that many Americans have difficulty comprehending. Give us a moment of time, and we are compelled to fill it with sound waves. That's why the title of this book is so American. If nothing else makes our time worthwhile, we at least ought to be able to *say* something. "Don't just stand there; say something" is an American coinage.

So, when we are confronted with the situation of visiting a person in a nursing home whose once brilliant mind is now reduced to the level of a three-year-old, we are hit with a double impact. Even if we did know what to say, it wouldn't make much difference because the person we are visiting probably wouldn't understand our words anyway.

But worse still, we really don't know what to say. What rational sense is there in a world where once intelligent people now spend five or ten years in what seems utter uselessness? And then when we stop to think that this might happen to us too, that's reason enough to be struck mute.

We need to get acquainted with the concept of mystery and ponder it. It will never make sense to an atheist or an agnostic except to give him or her more reason to rail against the injustice of God. But isn't it strange that when they either believe in God not at all or with the greatest difficulty, they have a strong conviction of what God ought to be like if God existed?

The Bible has some choice passages on mystery. Isaiah 55:8-9 says:

> "For my thoughts are not your thoughts,
>   neither are your ways my ways,"
>   declares the LORD.
> "As the heavens are higher than the earth,
>   so are my ways higher than your ways
> and my thoughts than your thoughts."

The aristocratic and intelligent Nicodemus was astounded at Jesus' words, "Flesh gives birth to flesh, but the Spirit gives birth to spirit. You should not be surprised at my saying, 'You must be born again.' The wind blows wherever it pleases. You hear its sound, but you cannot tell where it comes from or where it is going. So it is with everyone born of the Spirit." Nicodemus could only reply, "How can this be?"

Jesus replied, "You are Israel's teacher, and do not understand these things? I tell you the truth, we speak of what we know, and testify to what we have seen; but still you people do not accept our testimony. I have spoken to you of earthly things and you do not believe; how then will you believe if I speak of heavenly things?"

Sooner or later we have to learn that from a human viewpoint some things just don't make sense. One of those things is a nursing home day room full of people who were once proud and intelligent and cultured now sitting in wheelchairs, weak and debilitated.

Perhaps our visit with nursing home residents is as much for our sake as for theirs, to give us time to ponder some mysteries, even the mystery so contrary to our makeup that we are struck speechless. Silence may be more powerful than anything we can say.

Even when we don't know what to say, or if we have the feeling that what we do say is mundane and senseless, let's not think that we have failed to accomplish anything. We have been in the residents' company, and we have felt concern and love for them.

What do we say? Sometimes we may say nothing and thereby still communicate something about *being,* which may be more important than *saying.* We might choose to play along with a woman's fantasy that the President of the United States has visited her or that she has walked on the moon, letting her enjoy such mental adventures and loving her as we would love a child.

This may be another example of Knud Knudsen's sculpture that the helper is helped. In our effort to bring something to a resident of a nursing home, we may be the one who is blessed by the thoughts that come to our minds.

Don't overlook the possibility that the visit to a nursing home resident can be a truly inspirational experience. Sometimes we can tap the wealth of experience those residents have. Some may indeed become rather garrulous and talk on and on about things inconsequential. Others, however, may bring stories into the conversation that genuinely hold your attention.

Younger people, even teenagers, who generally are thought of as being very uncomfortable in visiting a nursing home, may find the experience fascinating as they learn what it was like to have left their home in Europe at the age of 13, never to see their parents again.

The inclusion of this chapter in this book is illustrative of changing times and changing situations. A generation or two ago, placing someone in a nursing home was often a depressing experience. It is still not a pleasant task and usually is not the preferred course of action. But there are times when it is the best alternative.

Also, there has come a greater appreciation for what people in care centers and nursing homes can mean to us. Encouraging them to tell stories from their earlier years can be an affirming experience for them and an enriching one for us.

7

What to Say in a Variety of Circumstances

This book could be extended to thirty or forty chapters, each one devoted to a specific situation in which it is difficult to know what to say. Some of the basic principles to guide conversation have been suggested in earlier chapters and can serve as guidelines in most situations.

Remember that there is no set formula for memorizing and saying precisely correct words for every specific occasion. There is no substitute for common sense and sensitivity developed by trying to place ourselves in the other person's shoes. And since other persons' shoes come in all sizes, we need to be flexible to adapt to the situation.

Not only is it difficult to find the right words when a tragedy has befallen someone, but sometimes it is equally awkward to know what to say when good fortune has come to someone. For instance, what do we say when someone has just had a job promotion, particularly when we also had hoped for a promotion and didn't get it? Can we be truly happy for someone else?

This chapter, then, will deal with a variety of circumstances in which you may feel you should say something but don't know quite what to say.

Mental Illness

First, let's look at some things that one might say when talking to family members of someone who is mentally ill. It is important to remember that there is a difference between being mentally retarded and mentally ill. Both present problems, and the families of either suffer pain. A mentally retarded person is one who from birth has had a below-average level of intelligence so that living normally as other people would is difficult. The severely retarded will probably not be able to live independently. Others, not as severely retarded, can live in group homes and, in the proper kind of environment, can lead satisfying lives.

Mental illness can afflict persons who are quite brilliant. All at once a chemical imbalance in the brain or some other malady strikes them so that at times they need to be hospitalized.

Here are some comments from parents whose son became mentally ill while in college, where he was an excellent student, but later had to be hospitalized frequently.

Like any other trauma that involves deep pain and suffering, those involved need to be approached with tenderness and care. There is often the added stigma that families believe that they are somehow guilty because their son or daughter has this illness.

People need to be willing to enter into the suffering of those families who have a member who is ill. If they are not prepared for that, they should not seek to converse in any depth with them. Such words as, "I know you are going through some very difficult times, and I would like to listen if you want to talk," might be a good opener. "I really don't know much about mental illness, but I'd like to learn and stand with you at this time," might be another.

If a person has had some experience with someone in his or her own family, an opener might be, "I think I know a little of your pain. My mother [brother, aunt, friend] struggles with mental illness." It is important for people not to assume that they know something about mental illness because their neighbor has a child who is mentally retarded. It is far better to admit ignorance as a conversation starter than to assume knowledge about something one knows very little about. If you encourage the family to share their experience and their knowledge, you are going to develop a rapport and relationship much more quickly. They may not want to talk right now, but give them the chance to tell you that. Don't assume it without asking. Perceptive questions that indicate attention to their feelings bring the most immediate and deepest response. "How are you *really* doing?" said with sincerity gives them the option to respond according to their needs.

This same person gave the following suggestions for talking to someone who is mentally ill:

In talking with the person who is ill, it is important to be as natural and normal as possible. Some *positive* comment about the person's appearance, surroundings, or something the person has done would be a good starter. The conversation may be shifted quickly by the ill person to himself or herself. It is important to listen but not to be drawn into giving advice or to try to pursue some therapeutic route. It may be good to shift the conversation away from the person who is ill if he seems to dwell on himself. After a relationship has been established, the ill person may want to use friends as a reality check. It is important then to be very honest and tell the ill person that what he thinks may be true for him does not match up with what we know. For instance, it might be important to say to a person, "I know your mind may be telling you that you are Jesus Christ, but I believe Christ lived and died and now continues to live in our world. You are a very important person to God, just as we all are."

It is extremely difficult for mentally ill persons to make and keep friends. They need normal friends who can enable them to live better and cope with the terrible things going on in their minds.

Alcohol and Drug Addiction

Two other complex problems that bring pain to many families are alcoholism and drug addiction. What do you say to a family while they are going through this pain? It all depends, of course, on what your relationship is with that family. Are they neighbors or close friends or relatives? Has it become publicly obvious that there is a problem, or is it still being hidden?

As in most instances, there is no set formula as to what you should say. The most important thing is attitude. A self-righteous, judgmental attitude will certainly not be helpful to the person or family involved. There was a time when it was thought that addiction was simply a matter of a weak will. The attitude was, "They could quit drinking if they really wanted to." Some people still hold that view. For them, to suggest that alcoholism might be a disease would only encourage the chemically dependent to excuse their behavior and continue in it.

While we still don't know all there is to know about alcoholism or drugs, there is at least evidence that these addictions are very complex.

Such opening statement as, "Is Jim having a problem?" asked in a nonjudgmental and caring way, can go a long way in beginning a conversation. Or "I'd really like to talk with you about . . ." spoken with a caring attitude can bring the kind of response that will enable you to know if the conversation can be continued with "Has she been in for some testing?" or "There are some helpful and hopeful treatments available these days."

One person who had an alcoholic son suggested that it is useful for families to go through the Al-Anon program even though the one addicted is not in or refuses treatment. "The experience can be very wholesome for the whole family," she said.

Other Difficult Situations

Other situations that raise the question, "What do you say when . . . ?" include:

- When you see your neighbor across the street for the first time after you have just learned that her unmarried daughter is pregnant?
- When a close friend is devastated because her son has just made it public that he is gay?
- When your neighbors have had a financial misfortune and have had to declare bankruptcy?
- When other neighbors have just lost their farm?
- When your friends have just had a baby with a severe birth defect?
- When your friends have experienced a miscarriage?
- When a son of close friends has been sent to prison?
- When a relative has been arrested for selling drugs?
- When a close friend has lost a job?

In some of these cases you may have a strong feeling that the action of your friends or members of their families went against your morals or standards, but you still want to be supportive of them during this difficult period. What do you say? Some of the phrases or sentences that follow may be helpful to you. Be sure to let the person talk whenever he or she wants to.

An unmarried daughter of a friend is pregnant. "Margaret, I heard about Sarah. I just want you to know that we love her and we love you. It's not for me to assess blame. Young people are going through difficult times these days. How is she doing, and how are you doing? Is there anything I can do?"

A son or daughter of a close friend announces that he or she is gay. This situation is fraught with so much emotion that many people have great difficulty dealing with it. In the first place, you may not be correct in assuming that it is public knowledge, so for you to bring up the subject, even in a very sensitive way, may take the parent by surprise. The parents may have shared the information with only a very few people, and with them in great confidence. For you now to broach the subject may make them feel that someone has betrayed their confidence.

Yet the parents may really want to talk to someone about their child. One way you can let it be known that you are open to such conversation without passing judgment is in other casual conversation—without referring to their son or daughter. You might talk about changing times and various life-styles and say that you yourself have been struggling in trying to understand them. This may open the door for your friends to talk with you about their child.

If they begin the conversation, you can continue with, "I'm honored that you trust me enough to talk about this, for I know that it is a difficult subject for many people. How did you feel when you found out about it?

How did [name] go about telling you? It is probably difficult for us to appreciate the struggle your son [or daughter] must have gone through."

Also, be sure to ask them if they want the information to be kept confidential at this time.

Financial misfortune. "Chuck, you've had a rough time. I've been thinking about you. I was so sorry to hear about your difficulty. Do you have any plans for the next step? Can I help you make any contacts?"

The lost farm. "This has got to be hard, Dave. I know the farm has been in your family for at least three generations. I can't begin to understand the feelings you must have. If you want to talk about it sometime, please come over. Let's not give up hope for the future."

A birth defect. "Maureen, I'm so sorry to hear about Jamie's problem. I wish I knew what more to say. Spina bifida is one of the great mysteries for medicine. I would guess that right now you don't know what to say either. How can Frank and I be of help? How is Mark taking it? I know he had looked forward to having a healthy boy who could play hockey with him."

The following is an excerpt from the column, "Dear Abby." The letter is from a mother whose baby, Anna, was born with spina bifida.

I can't tell you how many mass bouquets and sympathy cards we received—messages I consider inappropriate. I am still waiting to hear from friends who I suspect also "don't know what to say."

We have never been disappointed—Anna fits right into our family environment and is loved and cherished as much as her sister.

To those who are unsure how to react, do everything you would have done had the baby arrived without a problem. Don't assume that the parents are distraught and disappointed. Handicapped kids very often bring with them enormous amounts of joy and rewards. We think Anna is extra-special and feel privileged to welcome her into our family.

—Happy mother in California

A miscarriage. "Nancy, I was so sorry to hear the sad news. I know how much you and Richard wanted this baby. I feel so bad that it happened. Is there anything I can do?"

A son is sent to prison. "Lois, it has to be devastating to have Tim sent to prison. Be assured of our support for you. What can we do to ease the pain and the burden? Several in our church group are concerned and want to be helpful in whatever way we can."

A relative is caught selling drugs. "It's difficult these days, isn't it, with the pressure that is being put on kids. Did it come as a surprise to you, or had you known that Jim was involved in this? Do you know yet what the court and the police intend to do? Please know that we will stand by you during these hard days."

A friend has lost her job. "Denise, I hear you're one of those who got a pink slip. What are your plans? Is the company giving you good severance pay? I have been thinking about you a lot these days."

A major block in knowing what to say to people in seemingly awkward circumstances is our fear that they may think it is awkward, that they would rather not talk about it. The truth of the matter is that most people are hungering for some kind of recognition that they are hurting. The fact that you care about them often overwhelms them, and talking with them will usually not be as difficult as you suspect. You both will feel good about your having done so, and the more you do it, the easier it will become.

8

Religious Faith in Times of Crisis

S ome readers may be concerned that thus far this book has not said much about matters of faith. There have been some references to the Bible, including quotations from Psalms, Ecclesiastes, and Isaiah. There also was a warning not to impose our religious views on others during times of crisis. Earlier it was pointed out that many people have problems with mystery, and mystery is one of the components of religion.

For many people religious faith is closely related to crisis, either as a source of strength that sees them through a crisis or as a path to disappointment because their faith has not preserved them from crisis.

The phenomenal sale of Rabbi Harold Kushner's book *When Bad Things Happen to Good People* (New York: Schocken Books, 1981) testifies to both the universality of the question and the overwhelming comfort that many people find in their religious faith.

But because religion deals with mystery, it impresses us with our finiteness and therefore our inability to have all the answers. Times of crisis can lead to a feeling of awkwardness since many people have trouble talking about their faith. Furthermore, because we usually are somewhat uncertain as to how comfortable the person to whom we are talking at the time of crisis is with the subject, we are hesitant in knowing what to say.

For some people religion and a scriptural vocabulary are a part of everyday language. Daily prayer is a regular occasion for them. They feel so at ease with prayer that it would be quite appropriate for them to pray with the person in crisis and quote some Scripture verses. Not to do so almost would seem like a betrayal of faith, and they would be likely to feel guilty. They can point to instances where their particular witness has indeed brought strength in time of crisis, even to people who ordinarily were not religious. They may be particularly concerned—perhaps even surprised—that this book has not placed more emphasis on the resources of religious faith when one tries to bring consolation to the bereaved or strength to those in crisis. For them, this should have been the first chapter of the book.

But even these people need to be open to at least two cautions. First, a deep religious faith does not automatically shield them from grief or even resentment against God when death or terminal illness or other forms of distress strike. In fact, there is something wholesome about grief, and a denial of the opportunity for grieving may result in longer-lasting, deep-seated problems.

Several years ago a newspaper told about a funeral of a teenager who had been murdered in a particularly brutal way. The family was deeply religious, and their faith provided unusual strength to see them through this trying period. The funeral became a time of joy, because they were convinced that their child was now free from the sufferings of this earth and was in heaven where there would be no more suffering.

However, a medical doctor with years of experience in dealing with death expressed some concern over all the smiling faces at the funeral, even though he also had a strong faith and shared the feeling of the parents that their child was now in a better place.

"It seemed to me," he said, "that they were denying the opportunity for grieving. Grieving is necessary and it takes time, and while it may not always be accompanied by uncontrollable sobbing, it can hardly be done without a touch of sadness."

The other caution to people of deep faith at a time of crisis is not to be surprised that they are angry with God and express that anger with strong words. Anger with God and religious faith are not necessarily opposites. As noted earlier, the Bible tells of people who have definite complaints against God. These often are the very same people who also express a strong trust in God. It would be tragic therefore if this natural reaction of anger against God would cause people to call their own faith into question or the faith of people whom they are trying to comfort.

Perhaps timing is the most important factor in using religious language when trying to bring comfort to the distressed. Some people may indeed be comforted by a certain understanding that God can bring some good out of the tragedy that has happened to them. Aside from the fact that many people may have problems with that idea, even those who are comfortable with it may not want to hear it immediately following the tragedy.

Some think that a case can be made for even great tragedies being "the will of God." In his fifty-page book, *The Will of God* (Nashville: Abingdon, 1976), Leslie D. Weatherhead speaks of the will of God in three categories: the *intentional* will of God, the *circumstantial* will of God, and the *ultimate* will of God.

He uses the following illustration to explain his point: During World War II a man may have said that he was glad his son was a soldier, but that may not have been his original choice. He may have preferred that his son be a medical doctor or an architect. That would have been his intention. But under the circumstances of a Hitler loose in the world, endangering perhaps all of Western civilization, this man was glad that his son committed his life to fighting for freedom. In that sense, "under those circumstances," he could say that he was glad his son was a soldier. The ultimate result of this, he hoped, would be that Europe once again would be made free.

In a similar way it could be said that the *intentional* will of God is that everyone should experience only good. It was not God's intention that a 35-year-old mother with small children should die of cancer. But God made a stable universe operating according to stable and dependable laws. A bullet shot at a man will not suddenly swerve and go around him instead of hitting him if he is a Christian. A car gone out of control on ice will not suddenly stop before going over an embankment into fifty feet of water just because the driver is a Christian. The world operates by natural laws that are not any less divine because they are natural. In fact, natural laws themselves are a creation of God so that actions and reactions can be predicted with dependability.

Under circumstances of that kind it could be said that a tragedy may be "the will of God," God allowing something to happen because that is the way the world is put together. To say then that a tragedy is the *circumstantial* will of God is not so much a comfort, a saying of a positive thing about God, as it is simply a recognition of an imperfect world, the price we have to pay for being creatures with a free will. In a sense, then, one might say that a tragedy is the will of God but only the circumstantial will of God, something that God allows to happen under the circumstances of an imperfect world.

Weatherhead defines the *ultimate* will of God as the final realization of God's purpose, a bringing of the ultimate will of God in line with God's intentional will. This is the message of the Christian faith that ultimately God's will will be done and it will be good. This may be a rather empty promise to someone in the middle of a tragedy, and therefore one should not glibly hold it out, at least not in the first few words one feels called upon to say when visiting a family who has just experienced a tragic death or a woman who has just been told she has three months to live. It is, however, something that can be kept in the back of the mind for some future, more in-depth conversation.

Even when praying and hoping for a miracle, we need to be totally honest. Sometimes we may have a tendency to want to protect God by proclaiming God's power when the evidence on which we base our comments simply isn't there.

One man told how irritated he was when his minister continued to bring communion to his wife who by this time was virtually vegetative. The minister, telling about it afterward, would often comment, "It's always so uplifting to visit Marie at her bedside and give her communion. The strength of her faith shows through, as with strong hands she reaches out and guides the chalice to her mouth." The husband himself had been there many times and had never observed the same strength. He was ministered to more by the mystery of weakness than by the evidence of strength.

This is not to say that there are not times when there is an amazing show of strength that comes through in an almost miraculous way as a sick person responds to prayer and sacrament. But it is to say that, even if those signs are not there, that should not be taken to mean that God is not there. We do not need to come to God's rescue by proving God's presence with visible support. Those who have faith are not dependent on visible proof, and those who don't have faith will not be persuaded no matter how visible the "proof" may be.

In no sense am I trying to say that one should not rely on prayer and the comfort that comes from Bible verses in times of stress. For some people prayer comes very easily, and they are able to offer prayer, to listen and to benefit from others' prayers. For others it is more difficult.

A faithful Christian need not feel guilty, however, if his or her makeup is such that he or she does not feel comfortable to offer a prayer or "to say spiritual things." The awesomeness of tragedy is often so great that the very silence is evidence of sharing in the pain.

The prayer and Bible reading that is most satisfying and most "productive" may be that in which you engage after you get home from the visit, either alone or in a gathering of friends also acquainted with the tragedy. This experience will strengthen your own faith as well as establish a channel through which God's healing power can flow to the person who is grieving or in distress.

As you ponder the mysteries of God, some Scripture passages that may speak to you are these:

" '. . . For my thoughts are not your thoughts, neither are your ways my ways,' declares the LORD. 'As the heavens are higher than the earth, so are my ways higher than your ways and my thoughts than your thoughts' " (Isa. 55:8-9).

"For I am convinced that neither death nor life, neither angels nor demons, neither the present nor the future, nor any powers, neither height nor depth, nor anything else in all creation, will be able to separate us from the love of God that is in Christ Jesus our Lord" (Rom. 8:38-39).

"Do not let your hearts be troubled. Trust in God; trust also in me. In my Father's house are many rooms; if it were not so, I would have told you. I am going there to prepare a place for you. And if I go and prepare a place for you, I will come back and take you to be with me that you also may be where I am" (John 14:1-4).

"I am the resurrection and the life. He who believes in me will live, even though he dies; and whoever lives and believes in me will never die" (John 11:25-26).

"God is our refuge and strength, an ever-present help in trouble. Therefore we will not fear, though the earth give way and the mountains fall into the heart of the sea, though its waters roar and foam and the mountains quake with their surging" (Ps. 46:1-3).

"Now the dwelling of God is with men, and he will live with them. He will wipe every tear from their eyes. There will be no more mourning nor crying nor pain, for the old order of things has passed away."

(Rev. 21:3-4)

Many other Scripture passages are rich with comfort, strength, and meaning. Many of the Psalms are particularly strengthening and comforting.

The occasion itself will call forth numerous specific prayers for yourself as well as for others. Most of them may be short cries for help: "O God, help me: help me to say the right thing." "God, be with Bill and Joan during these difficult times. Give them wisdom, insight, and patience." "God, I don't understand all of this, but I leave it in your hands." You may learn again the mystery of intercessory prayer, how God often answers your prayers for someone else.

Then there are the many classic prayers, formally and carefully worded, that have been prayed by saints through the centuries. These may be too formal to pray with the person you are trying to comfort, particularly if there are other people present. But the occasion itself may drive you to be more open to prayer in general, not just relating to the situation at hand, but finding a sustaining power for all circumstances of life.

We sometimes feel that books of written prayers are not as meaningful as those that spring out of our own depth during times of tragedy. However, they can at times give us a greater perspective on life. The following prayers, taken from *Lutheran Book of Worship (LBW)* and *Service Book and Hymnal (SBH),* may not deal with the precise situations that called forth the prayer in the first place; but having been put in the mood of prayer by your or someone else's tragedy, they can be enriching:

Lord God, you have called your servants to ventures of which we cannot see the ending, by paths as yet untrodden, through perils unknown. Give us faith to go out with good courage, not knowing where we go, but only that your hand is leading us and your love supporting us; through Jesus Christ our Lord. Amen. (LBW)

Have compassion, O Lord, upon all who mourn and upon all who are lonely and desolate; be thou their

Comforter and Friend; give them such earthly solace as thou seest to be best for them; bring them to fuller knowledge of thy love; and wipe away all their tears; for the sake of Jesus Christ our Lord. Amen. (SBH)

Almighty and everlasting God, the comfort of the sad, the strength of them that suffer: Let the prayers of thy children who cry out of any tribulation come unto thee; and unto every soul that is distressed grant thou mercy, grant relief, grant refreshment. Amen. (SBH)

O God, who hast drawn over the weary day the restful veil of night, enfold us in thy heavenly peace. Lift from our hands our tasks, and bear in thy bosom the weight of our burdens and sorrows; that in untroubled slumber we may press our weariness close to thy strength, and win from thee new power for the morrow's labors. Amen. (SBH)

Watch thou, dear Lord, with those who wake, or watch, or weep tonight, and give thine angels charge over those who sleep. Tend thy sick ones, O Lord. Rest thy weary ones. Bless thy dying ones. Soothe thy suffering ones. Pity thine afflicted ones. Shield thy joyous ones. And grant all for thy love's sake, in Jesus Christ our Lord. Amen. (LBW)

O Lord, support us all the day long of this troubled life, until the shadows lengthen, and the evening comes, and the busy world is hushed, and the fever of life is over, and our work is done. Then in thy mercy, grant us a safe lodging and a holy rest, and peace at last. Amen. (LBW)

Afterword

From Saying to Doing to Growing

What started out as an attempt to give some very practical suggestions in various trying circumstances about what a person ought to say has brought us full circle to realize that perhaps "saying" isn't the most important thing after all. Neither, however, do we want to minimize what is said. Words are powerful. They can uplift and they can destroy. One should be commended for trying to say the right words.

But when we come up against difficult and tragic situations and feel called upon to say something, there is seldom time to take a course in appropriate things to say. The purpose of this book was not to give such a course, least of all to make us specialists in what to say or to become professional counselors. The most I hoped for was that it might give some suggestions that would put persons at a little greater ease in knowing what to say.

Important as words are, there come times when the situation is so overwhelming that we need to give equal attention to silence on the one hand and action on the other. At times the greatest consolation we can bring to a person suffering tragedy is simply our presence and thereby the assurance of our caring—a touch on the arm, a strong embrace, shedding tears together. Furthermore, the tentacles of tragedy are far-reaching. Although a quick pain reliever may be in order, the pain will come back. A commitment to caring carries with it a long-term commitment to action.

On several occasions the book made reference to a bronze statue by Knud Knudsen, a German sculptor, which carries with it the message that the helper is often the one who is helped the most. Participating in tragedies of others and bringing healing balm often enriches the one trying to bring comfort. The helper himself or herself is helped by developing a greater appreciation for the mystery of suffering and being driven to the One who is all powerful.

Growth takes place with each act of caring, so with each new trying circumstance, you will find it just a bit easier to know what to do and say.

Bibliography

Brandt, Leslie F. *Bible Readings for Troubled Times.* Minneapolis: Augsburg, 1984.

Davidson, Glen W. *Living with Dying: A Guide for Relatives and Friends.* Minneapolis: Augsburg, 1989.

————. *Understanding Mourning.* Minneapolis: Augsburg, 1984.

Erickson, Kenneth A. *Please, Lord, Untie My Tongue.* St. Louis: Concordia, 1983.

Haugk, Kenneth. *Christian Caregiving: A Way of Life.* Minneapolis: Augsburg, 1984.

Kübler-Ross, Elisabeth. *On Death and Dying.* New York: Macmillan, 1970.

Kuenning, Delores. *Helping People through Grief.* Minneapolis: Bethany House, 1987.

Kushner, Harold S. *When Bad Things Happen to Good People.* New York: Shocken Books, 1981.

Palms, Roger C. *Bible Readings on Hope.* Minneapolis: Augsburg, 1987.

Rogness, Alvin N. *Book of Comfort.* Minneapolis: Augsburg, 1979.

————. *My Personal Prayer Book.* Minneapolis: Augsburg, 1988.

Schuchardt, Erika. *Why Is This Happening to Me?: Guidance and Hope for Those Who Suffer.* Minneapolis: Augsburg, 1989.

Syverson, Betty Groth. *Bible Readings for Caregivers.* Minneapolis: Augsburg, 1987.

Weatherhead, Leslie D. *The Will of God.* Nashville: Abingdon, 1941, 1972.

Westberg, Granger E. *Good Grief.* Minneapolis: Fortress Press, 1962, 1971.

Williams, Philip W. *When a Loved One Dies.* Minneapolis: Augsburg, 1976.